AF335606

MUSIC:
A Suite & Thirteen Songs

BOOKS/CHAPBOOKS BY KIRK ROBERTSON

The Burning Fire Chief (1975)
Shooting At Shadows, Killing Crows (1975)
Drinking Beer At 22 Below (1976)
Walked On By 40 Camels (1977)
Sultry Afternoon With The Blinds Partly Pulled (1978)
Shovel Off To Buffalo (1978)
Under The Weight Of The Sky (1978)
Coffee, Dust Devils & Old Rodeo Bulls (1979)
No Deposit, No Return (1980)
Nevada (1980)
Origins, Initiations (1980)
Reasons And Methods (1981)
West Nevada Waltz (1981)
Two Weeks Off (1977, 1984)
Art·i·facts (1985)
Matters Of Equal Height (1987)
Driving To Vegas: New & Selected Poems, 1969–87 (1989)
Music: A Suite & 13 Songs (1995)
Desert Saudade: Selected & New Poems, 1969–94
    (forthcoming, 1996)

MUSIC:
A Suite & Thirteen Songs

Kirk Robertson

A Great Basin Book
FLOATING ISLAND PUBLICATIONS
CEDARVILLE / CALIFORNIA
1995

ISBN: 0-912449-51-9

Published by:
Floating Island Publications
P.O. Box 341
Cedarville, California 96104

Some of these poems appeared in: *American Poets Say Goodbye To
The Twentieth Century* (Four Walls/Eight Windows); *Floating Island*;
Invisible City; *The Lahontan Valley News*; *New Work(s)* (Duck Down);
and, *Poetry NOW*.

"West Nevada Waltz" was originally published in a limited edition
by Turkey Press with original paper drawings by Harry Reese.

Cover photo is from Jack Fulton's series "Suite Nevada," which had
its origins in central Nevada in 1990.

for Valerie

Let us turn once more . . .
To the noise of insatiable movement

—Arthur Rimbaud

CONTENTS

Thirteen Songs

WEST NEVADA WALTZ:
A Suite of Poems

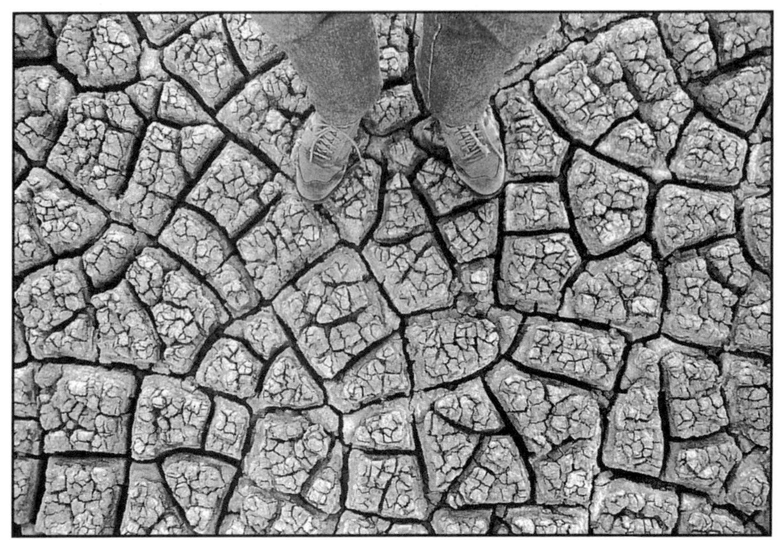

Going backwards, retracing your steps
looking for something you've lost

Something you had
at least thought you did
once

In the only theatre
of a small Nevada town
you watch the film begin to run
crazily back toward
its cannister

It is old and badly scratched
hard to see through
what appears to be
mustard colored rain

You cannot see
exactly what was going on
back there

But that's where you must have
lost something that you need now

The keys that will unlock
your door heat
the early morning dark

So you squint
and keep on looking

Clark and Marilyn are sitting in a bar
in Reno drinking doubles talking
about leaving not to any place in
particular just moving on getting out

The jukebox is spouting something
about hanging in and hanging on
like autumn leaves before they fall

It was true it would be an early
winter for although there were few
trees in Reno to shed their leaves
the honkers were already heading south
and it was only the 23rd of August

They could barely hear the music
above the dull mechanical roar
of the casino—a combination
of dollars dropped into slots
handles being pulled and bells
going off everytime someone put
in three and got two back

There were old women sitting on red
naugahyde stools pulling the handles
again and again with a slow desperate
assembly line familiarity as if
they had sat on those same stools
for twenty-five years

You know she says *I walked out*
to the city limits once   it didn't
look like much was out there

Clark kills his drink in one gulp
motions to the bartender to bring
them another round nods at her
and says *Yeah but it may be the*
only place there's anything left

They look at one another across
the table and something passes
between them like a sudden breeze
across the furnace of a Nevada afternoon

They leave the bar find his
battered pickup drive up Virginia
to 4th Street and then head east
into the desert leaving Reno
and a technicolor even in
black and white sunset
behind them

The Great Basin least spectacular
of all North American deserts and
almost the entire state is contained
within its boundaries

Where what would barely pass
elsewhere for a stream
is a river and none of them
will ever find the sea

Even so we have less water
and more desert around us
than anywhere else
including Arizona

The county has had more than seventy
towns come but because the ore
played out fire burned them out
or the water dried up only Fallon
continued to grow

Today the eastern county line is
not known exactly and the western edge
of Fallon reaches towards Reno
saying: Raley's   Sprouse-Reitz
Country Kitchen   Kentucky Fried
Chicken

But if you look at the *old* maps
and listen

You hear:

Bango *Bolivia*
Bell Flat *Bunejug Mountains*

Carson Sink *Cocoon Mountains*
Dixie Valley *Dead Camel Mountains*

Eastgate *Eightmile Flat*
Forty Mile Desert *Frenchman's*

Hard To Find Mine *Hazen*
Ione *Job's Peak*

La Plata *Middlegate*
Mirage *Mopung Hills*

Quicksilver Mine *Ragtown*
Salt Wells *Sand Mountain*

Seeho Springs *Stillwater*
Stinking Springs *Swingle Bench*

Westgate *White House Rock*
Wildcat Station *Wonder*

Yomba

It's really not that hard
to find although many have
passed by few stopped
fewer yet stayed

Not even the county seat
remained for long

It's not that everything
you need will be here
it's that so much you don't
will *not* be

So bring what you cannot
give up wanting
with you and think of it
as a place you're always
it seems either coming
from or going to

It's not that far
from where you are
right now calling
probably from
a bar uptown

And although it sometimes
looks out the window
an awfully lot like
it feels inside your head
before you adjust your
margins and put the paper in

Right now there are clouds
the color of the light
in the center or a glass
of white wine floating
around on the faded
blue levis of the sky

There are several things about
the weather around here that
you can more or less count on
among them heat cold and wind

It's rare to draw three
at once but a pair
is not unusual

Adding to the wind you draw
one of those winter come
back in late March days

On which you have to go
into Reno on *business*

And it's somewhere out around Mustang
or Painted Rock where it's gusting
at seventy or eighty miles an hour
there's an eighteen wheeler jack
knifed on the interstate and

The car heater going full tilt
can't hold off the cold

That you realize that you've
been here *right here*
before the feeling strikes
suddenly as they say
without warning

You see coming home
through the dust and tumbleweeds
the inverted reflections
of distant things grow closer

Last fall's leaves are sucked up
to float around and around
in front of you

And then although lightning's
not supposed to twice
you watch the sun
in your rear view mirror
drop into what you distinctly
remember as

The humming mosquito colored air
of a late last July afternoon

It's after midnight

For the first time
since seven this morning
you switch the cooler off

Just five minutes ago
and you're sweating already

What was left of the moon
finally came up

Too hot to sleep you turn on
the one channel you get
out here in the desert
John Wayne's lawless frontier
is all there is

110 today

Hotter tomorrow
the forecast calls
for *some* clouds

In the afternoon you'll
probably even wish for rain
just to cool things down
but you know it will not come
know also that you'll
have to wait it out

As the Ichthyosaurs must have

Drying up with the sea

Here
where the dark and the light
collide

Under the blankets of the sky

The mirror is chipped and pitted
its surface almost worn away
from the constant battering
of driven sand

The images look as if they
have been there a long time but
appear suddenly like middle age

The onset of arthritis at thirty-two
a desert wind on a ninety-nine degree day
you can actually see it moving
toward you

At first it doesn't look like
it will be *that* bad the climate
after all is supposed
to be good for it

Then you see from seventy miles away
a twelve foot woman on fire
and a man on trial for
shooting his four month old son

Finally its strength is too much
the saplings have all bent double
everything is layered with fine dust

You watch the tumbleweeds let go
roll with the rippling metal sound
mobile homes make on such a day
and for a while you're moving along

fairly well but any sudden intrusion
or marshalling of the facts
even small ones stretched thin
and taut as wire between fenceposts
hangs you up stops you are stuck
there so long even the smallest
amount of effort becomes too much

Though you can still hear it
coming from some distance off
like the by now only half remembered
song of her wind blown hair
moving across the desert's face

So you listen but no longer know
if this is the right place
or if like holding a door
or a coat it's just
a matter of being there
at the right time

Look even the curtains are dancing
straight out in the air almost
parallel to the floor

You've driven over
nine hundred miles
just to be here
for a few days
where it's warm enough
and dry enough
to sit on the porch
in the sun on the day
after Christmas
under a sky
you'd almost forgotten
could be blue

The few clouds
are so high and thin
that when they pass
in front of the sun
there's no change
in the light and
it takes a while
for you to feel
your shirt growing
cold against your skin

But the chill
passes quickly
like a first snow
that sticks around
only in the shadows
of the ditchbank

So you decide
to walk up and
get the mail
with the sky
the only coat
around you

Moving away

It takes a while for things
you thought lost to reappear
but sooner or later they do
and you find that the differences
are not ones of contrast
but the lack of it

Gone are salt white clouds
and deep azure sky *there*
things are more diffuse
less certain
a TV set with
no contrast
everything gray
muted

Once you left the desert's heat
to sit in front of the wood stove
most of the day trying to decide
which was the right piece
to burn next which would catch
and not fill the house with smoke

While through your window you watched
greens and blues even the blacks
of a moonless night bleed into gray
under the constant billowing rain

After five straight days it
finally let up and became
so foggy that even though
the softest sounds were amplified
they remained as distant
as the worn out feelings
of an old record

Warm

Under that late afternoon
in mid-February bright blue sky

With salsa in the kitchen
window full of immense blue
backed flat bottomed white clouds
sailing by honky tonks and
harsh lights on your radio

The air is as crisp
as the light

And you can see it coming
for miles and miles

Sneaking in and out
of the clouds as if
looking for someplace
better safer
to stash the loot

And finding no place better

Than right here

I learned how to listen
for a sound like the sun going down . . .

Rodney Crowell

It isn't so much a matter
of not looking a gift horse
in the mouth but rather
a matter of not looking
any horse in the mouth

Out here valleys are measured
in miles *across* and no matter
how long it takes out there
in the middle
under the sun
you like Fall always
seem to arrive
just *barely* in time

After a while there's no longer
enough left to waste
on crossing the damn things
just to see if it's any better
over there after all
are folks who've pretty
much decided the same thing

Somewhere along the line
even though there are those times
when like a horse tethered in one place
too long you reach the end of your rope
you begin to settle in

Begin to forget the orange cherry
orange combinations which didn't
pay off and noticing only how easily
the bright yellow leaves all around
this so-called oasis let go and
start to waltz towards the ground
you believing she just might
show up again

Begin to wait for the moon

Which like an expected check
always takes too long shows
up late stumbling
across the black ice of the sky
like a tipsy redhead in high heels
full but still in the 1980s
only worth a quarter

She's not much what with her makeup
smeared and all often looking the next
day like noontime neon—showing only
a hint of what she was the night before

But right now up there shimmering
almost dancing across that nimble
three-quarter time blue sky she looks
like the damndest schooner you
ever did see and of course

There are the clouds

THIRTEEN SONGS

for Valerie & for Jack Fulton

Dave saved up his money and bought a bar. He liked classical music and since the bar was in the middle of the Great Basin night miles from the likelihood to hear any such thing, he decided what the hell, called it the Mozart Club. He really couldn't remember whether it was Chopin, Satie, Mozart or Mendelssohn that had moved him so, but he liked the sound of Mozart. He painted a big skeleton on the side of the bar emblazoned with the legend, "This Guy Drank Water." A lot of local folks thought that was pretty funny and began to call the watering hole home.

Every month or so Dave and this painter friend of his would make the day-long drive to Reno on a supply run. They were at the Santa Fe and had consumed way too many picons and that great Friday night Basque steak dinner. They were standing around the bar drinking Winnemucca coffees, debating whether they should head back or not and if they did who, given all the picons, was the most qualified to drive, when she walked in.

She was the most drop-dead, beautiful woman they'd ever seen. She could have been northern Italian or English or Irish, what with that stunning mane of red hair and those amazing legs. But she was, in fact, Austrian. After a quick look around she walked to the end of the bar and sat on a stool, crossing her legs high. Dave, and everyone else in the bar, was speechless. She had silenced that rowdy, Friday night crowd just by walking in like the way, sometimes, the sun going down can stop a wind that's been howling all day across the desert's face.

Dave watched his heart tumble out of his chest and flop
around on the bar like some fish sensing that it was, after all,
the seventh year of a drought and this just might be it.

"Would you like a drink?" he suddenly blurted out.

Their eyes locked and that was it. They spent the next three
hours drinking at a small table in the back. Dave kept feeding
her small slices of lime from the palm of his hand and she'd
laugh, oh how she'd laugh. She'd get up every so often to go
and call someone and Dave would watch her walk to the
phone and back wondering, wondering. . . . He even reached
under the table once and squeezed her leg, thinking, oh my
God what a stupid thing to do, now she'll walk out and I'll
never see her again.

But she stayed and talked and drank and they both felt some kind
of furnace burning within them like never before until, finally,
she said, "I have to go. My brother's coming to pick me up."

She left with her brother. Dave left with his painter friend and
they all ended up standing in the parking lot, Dave and her
just staring at each other, neither wanting to break the
connection. "Jeezus Christ, Dave," the painter said, "Put your
goddamn eyes back in your head and open the goddamn door."

Who's to say what happened next or how it happened but
Dave hung around until he saw her again and that's all it took.
A done deal. Never a question. She came back to the Mozart
Club with him. That's when the music really began. And from
then on everyone kept commenting on how amazing it all was,
how right it all seemed, how good they looked together, how
glad they were for Dave.

This is it, Dave thought. At last. And he began to think of waltzing toward the millenium on a sea of melodious light. But then there's always life. It goes on, as they say. And it does. But it also can just suddenly stop.

He went down to the bar one day and came home to find her gone. No note. No word. Nothing. Her clothes, her shoes, everything but her, still there. Dave looked and looked, went back up to Reno, but nothing, not a trace. No one even knew her.

It was as if she had never existed, as if it had all never happened. But Dave knew it had and he tried to forget but couldn't because he didn't really want to forget. He never did look at another woman and he drank more than a bit and it was worse than fighting the weather, all that thinking about it, wondering what had happened, why there were all these years of nights they might have been together, but weren't.

It was thirty years later, almost to the day, that this gorgeous redhead walked into the Mozart Club. Everyone was stumbling over themselves, hitting on her, trying to buy her a drink, everyone that is but Dave, who just sat at the end of the bar nursing his drink. But she wasn't interested in all the attention and only wanted one thing.

"Is there anyone here named Dave?" she asked.

"Down there, end of the bar," Dave's painter friend said.

She walked down to the end of the bar, everyone watching her every move. "Dave?" she asked.

"Yeah?" he said, looking up from his drink, his bloodshot blues meeting her amber ones. "What'ya want?"

"I'm your daughter," she said.

And so the story was told. How her mother was from a very wealthy Austrian family; how she had come to the States on vacation with her brother; how she had walked into a bar in Reno one Friday night and fallen head-over-heels in love with the piercing blue eyes of a guy named Dave who owned a bar; how her grandmother had disowned her mother for having the audacity to do that; how after that it didn't seem to matter until her grandmother fell ill and wanted her daughter back home before she died; how her grandmother sent her son back to the States to kidnap her daughter; how her mother was in a car accident and they were able to save the baby, but not her; how her grandmother recovered, raised her and never mentioned any of it; how her uncle told her all about it only after her grandmother finally died.

Who could have known
that it would whip

Your hair to a frenzy
provoking fantasies

Of what it might
be like to be

Tangled there
heat from your eyes

Shimmering toward me
across the parking lot

What happened there
afterwards

I never felt the same
not ever

Not

Ever again

RIMBAUD STOPS AT THE LIQUOR STORE IN MOJAVE

The wind with so little
to hold its interest

Is making speeches
about her hair

The sky's full
of stained cotton fleece

The sound of drunken boats
filling the air

And nothing
nothing made much sense

Without her

The bigger the hat

The smaller the ranch

Could be Butte Tonopah
Livingston or Lamoille

It's all about the same

In late January
rust pitted pickups
bounce around
3:00 AM chuckholes

Passenger doors
swinging open wide

Honey, I'm sorry
would you please
just get back
in the truck

The mistake always
trying to word it
too soon

The regret always
in not having
done it sooner

THINKING ABOUT YOU, READING CREELEY

Three hundred miles into
the midst of a Great Basin night

February thoughts of your red lips
tumble through my mind

Errors accumulate like late snow
in a high desert ditch bank

Building out of our sight
the terrible thoughts of time

*What did I know thinking myself
able to go alone all the way*

She thinks about swaying to Joe Ely
he thinks Leonard Cohen's lyrics
when she suddenly turns to him
asks about the words to *Suzanne*

January quickly becomes July
around here what you plants

Comes in spades

Or not at all

Spring fully sprung
again

I find myself
talking

To this year's leaves
about

Exactly the same
things

I spoke of

To last year's

Standing by the fence
listening to low down blues

Fireworks over Rattlesnake pale
fade in comparison

To the blaze
of your pink dress

Glowing against
the oncoming obsidian night

I remember Lew Welch's line
about Muses and Mistresses

About confusion
about trouble

And I thought I knew
what he meant

Until the wind
from your hair

Blew both my way

I've been thinking
bout nothing but you

For two straight days
your voice

The memory the fire
of your touch

Becoming liquid
sounds like the scroop
of your skirt

As you descend
the staircase take
me in your mouth

Becoming the liquid
line drawn by my tongue
through your delta

Sounds
so much like music

Sliding into you
that even the rain
bursts into flame

VALERIE & KIRK / PHOTO BY JACK FULTON

Kirk Robertson is a poet and visual artist and has lived in Fallon, Nevada since 1976. He has published 18 books/chapbooks of poetry and a new collection *Desert Saudade: Selected & New Poems 1969–94* is forthcoming from the University of Nevada Press in 1996. He is also a consultant to the Churchill Arts Council, a columnist for the *Lahontan Valley News* and editor of *neon*, the journal of the Nevada State Council on the Arts.

COLOPHON

Published in an edition of 1000 copies in the Spring of 1995 by
Floating Island Publications in Cedarville, California. Printed and
bound by McNaughton & Gunn, Inc., of Ann Arbor, Michigan.
Cover photograph and art by Jack Fulton. Photographs in the text
by Michael Sykes. Designed, typeset and produced at Archetype
West, Point Reyes Station, California by Michael Sykes. The
typeface for the text is Goudy Old Style, composed on an ancient
Compugraphic Editwriter 7500 and all mechanicals done by hand.

Barn Fires by Peter Wild

Desemboque by Frank Graziano

Sleeping With The Enemy by Christina Zawadiwsky

The Golden Legend by Jeffery Beam

Up My Coast by Joanne Kyger

The Open Water by Frank Stewart

Dazzled by Arthur Sze

Drug Abuse in Marin County by Eugene Lesser

Black Ash, Orange Fire by William Witherup

Flying the Red Eye by Frank Stewart

Point Reyes Poems by Robert Bly

Ordinary Messengers by Michael Hannon

Seminary Poems by Diane di Prima

Park by Cole Swensen

The Raven Wakes Me Up by Stephan Torre

Blue Skies by Robert Fromberg

Ten Poems by Issa, English Versions by Robert Bly

Sheet of Glass by Stefanie Marlis

Cazadero Poems by Susan Kennedey & Mike Tuggle

Winter Channels by James Schevill

Poetry Is Dangerous by Tony Moffeit